Bible Journeys in 40 Days

Day 1: In the Beginning
Day 2: The Fall of Man
Day 3: Noah and the Flood
Day 4: The Call of Abram
Day 5: Isaac and Rebekah
Day 6: Jacob and Esau
Day 7: Joseph's Dreams
Day 8: Moses and the Burning Bush
Day 9: The Ten Plagues
Day 10: The Exodus and the Red Sea
Day 11: The Ten Commandments
Day 12: The Promised Land
Day 13: Gideon's Victory
Day 14: Samson's Strength
Day 15: Ruth's Loyalty
Day 16: The Anointing of King David
Day 17: David and Goliath
Day 18: Solomon's Wisdom
Day 19: Elijah and the Prophets of Baal
Day 20: Elisha's Miracles
Day 21: Jonah and the Great Fish
Day 22: Isaiah's Prophecies
Day 23: Daniel in the Lion's Den
Day 24: The Birth of Jesus
Day 25: Jesus' Baptism and Temptation
Day 26: The Sermon on the Mount
Day 27: Jesus' Miracles and Teachings
Day 28: The Parables of Jesus
Day 29: The Transfiguration
Day 30: The Last Supper
Day 31: The Crucifixion
Day 32: The Resurrection
Day 33: The Great Commission
Day 34: The Ascension
Day 35: The Day of Pentecost
Day 36: Paul's Conversion
Day 37: The Early Church
Day 38: The Missionary Journeys of Paul
Day 39: The Fruit of the Spirit
Day 40: The Second Coming of Christ

A Life-Changing Journey

Welcome to 40 Days Through the Bible: A Journey to Fulfillment. This transformative Bible study invites you to embark on a spiritual journey that will not only deepen your understanding of God's Word but also help you find meaning, purpose, and fulfillment in your life.

Over the next 40 days, you will explore some of the most significant stories and themes of the Bible, discovering how they apply to your own life and spiritual journey.

A Unique Approach to Bible Study

This book is designed to be both engaging and accessible, making it suitable for people of all ages, backgrounds, and levels of familiarity with the Bible.

The 40-day structure allows you to immerse yourself in the world of the Bible, while the daily devotionals and weekly reflections provide opportunities for personal growth, contemplation, and connection with God.

Each day, you will encounter a new theme or story from the Bible, accompanied by thought-provoking reflections, relevant Bible passages, practical applications, and heartfelt prayers.

The weekly reflections offer a more in-depth exploration of the themes covered, as well as additional Bible passages, activities, and discussion questions for personal or group use.

An Invitation to Spiritual Growth

At the heart of this book is an invitation to grow closer to God and to discover His plan and purpose for your life. As you journey through the Bible, you will encounter timeless truths and powerful lessons that can transform your heart, mind, and soul.

You will also be challenged to apply these lessons to your daily life, seeking God's guidance and wisdom in every situation. Through prayer, meditation, and reflection, you will learn to depend on God's strength and grace and to embrace His call to live a life of fulfillment and purpose.

A Community of Believers

While this book is designed for individual study, it can also be used as a tool for building community and fostering spiritual growth among groups of believers.

Whether you are participating in a small group, a Bible study class, or a church-wide program, you will find that this book provides a framework for meaningful conversations, shared experiences, and spiritual growth.

As you journey through the Bible together, you will be encouraged to support and uplift one another, to hold each other accountable, and to pray for each other. In this way, you will not only deepen your understanding of God's Word but also strengthen the bonds of fellowship and love that unite you as the body of Christ.

Embracing the Adventure

As you embark on this 40-day journey through the Bible, remember that you are not alone. God is with you every step of the way, guiding, empowering, and equipping you to face the challenges and opportunities that lie ahead.

And as you seek His face and delve into His Word, you will find that He is indeed the source of all meaning, purpose, and fulfillment.

So, open your heart and mind to the life-changing message of the Bible, and prepare to embark on an adventure that will transform your life and deepen your relationship with God.

May your journey be filled with joy, discovery, and growth, and may you be forever changed by the power of God's Word.

Welcome to Bible Journeys in 40 Days . Your adventure begins now!

Day 1: In the Beginning

Reflection

As we embark on our journey through the Bible, let us begin with the creation of the world.

Genesis 1:1 tells us, "In the beginning, God created the heavens and the earth."

Reflect on the magnificence and order of God's creation and consider the role you play in His grand design.

Bible Passage : Genesis 1:1-5 (NIV)

In the beginning, God created the heavens and the earth.

Now the earth was formless and empty, darkness was over the surface of the deep, and the Spirit of God was hovering over the waters.

And God said, "Let there be light," and there was light.

God saw that the light was good, and he separated the light from the darkness.

God called the light "day," and the darkness he called "night." And there was evening, and there was morning—the first day.

Application

Spend some time in nature today, observing the beauty and intricacy of God's creation.

Consider how you can be a better steward of the environment and the resources He has provided.

Lord Teach Me To	I Am Thankful For

Prayer

Heavenly Father, thank You for the wonder and beauty of Your creation.

Help me to appreciate and care for the world You have made, and to recognize my place in Your grand design. **Amen.**

Day 2: The Fall of Man

Reflection

In Genesis 3, we witness the fall of man as Adam and Eve disobey God and eat from the tree of knowledge of good and evil.

This pivotal moment in the Bible teaches us about sin, disobedience, and the consequences of our actions.

Reflect on times when you have strayed from God's path and consider how you can seek His forgiveness and guidance.

Bible Passage: Genesis 3:1-6 (NIV)

Now the serpent was more crafty than any of the wild animals the LORD God had made. He said to the woman, "Did God really say, 'You must not eat from any tree in the garden'?"

The woman said to the serpent, "We may eat fruit from the trees in the garden, but God did say, 'You must not eat fruit from the tree that is in the middle of the garden, and you must not touch it, or you will die.'"

"You will not certainly die," the serpent said to the woman.
"For God knows that when you eat from it your eyes will be opened, and you will be like God, knowing good and evil."

When the woman saw that the fruit of the tree was good for food and pleasing to the eye, and also desirable for gaining wisdom, she took some and ate it. She also gave some to her husband, who was with her, and he ate it.

Application

Identify a situation in your life where you need to seek forgiveness from God or someone else.

Take the necessary steps to make amends and learn from your mistakes.

Lord Teach Me To	I Am Thankful For

Prayer

Lord, forgive me for the times I have disobeyed You and strayed from Your path.

Help me to learn from my mistakes and to seek Your guidance in all that I do. **Amen.**

Day 3: Noah and the Flood

Reflection

As we continue our journey through the Bible, we come across the story of Noah and the Flood.

This account in Genesis 6-9 shows us the consequences of widespread sin and God's decision to cleanse the earth.

At the same time, it demonstrates God's mercy and grace, as He saves Noah and his family from the destruction.

Reflect on the concept of God's judgment, as well as His promise to never again destroy the earth in such a manner.

Bible Passage :   Genesis 6:9-14 (NIV)

This is the account of Noah and his family. Noah was a righteous man, blameless among the people of his time, and he walked faithfully with God. Noah had three sons: Shem, Ham, and Japheth.

Now the earth was corrupt in God's sight and was full of violence. God saw how corrupt the earth had become, for all the people on earth had corrupted their ways.

So God said to Noah, "I am going to put an end to all people, for the earth is filled with violence because of them. I am surely going to destroy both them and the earth.

So make yourself an ark of cypress wood; make rooms in it and coat it with pitch inside and out.

Application

Consider areas in your life where you may be contributing to the "corruption" of the world, whether through harmful thoughts, words, or actions.

Reflect on how you can make a positive change and walk more closely with God.

Lord Teach Me To	I Am Thankful For

Prayer

Heavenly Father, thank You for the story of Noah, which demonstrates both Your judgment and Your mercy.

Help me to recognize and address the areas in my life that may be displeasing to You, and guide me to walk faithfully in Your ways. **Amen.**

Day 4: The Call of Abram

Reflection

The call of Abram, later known as Abraham, is a significant moment in the Bible, as it marks the beginning of God's covenant with His chosen people.

Abram's faith in God and willingness to follow His command without question is a powerful example of trust and obedience.

Reflect on times when you have been called to follow God's direction, even when it seemed uncertain or challenging.

Bible Passage :   Genesis 12:1-4 (NIV)

The LORD had said to Abram, "Go from your country, your people, and your father's household to the land I will show you.

I will make you into a great nation, and I will bless you; I will make your name great, and you will be a blessing.

I will bless those who bless you, and whoever curses you I will curse; and all peoples on earth will be blessed through you."

So Abram went, as the LORD had told him; and Lot went with him. Abram was seventy-five years old when he set out from Harran.

Application

Identify a situation in your life where you may be feeling God's call to step out in faith.

Pray for guidance, strength, and the courage to trust in God's plan, even when it seems uncertain.

Lord Teach Me To	**I Am Thankful For**

Prayer

Lord, I ask for Your guidance and wisdom as I seek to follow Your call in my life.

Help me to trust in Your plan and to step out in faith, even when it is challenging or uncertain. **Amen.**

Day 5: Isaac and Rebekah

Reflection

The story of Isaac and Rebekah highlights God's divine guidance and providence in the lives of His people.

As you read about the circumstances that brought Isaac and Rebekah together, consider how God has worked in your own life to guide you to where you are today.

Reflect on the blessings and relationships in your life that are a result of God's hand at work.

Bible Passage : Genesis 24:61-67 (NIV)

Then Rebekah and her attendants got ready and mounted the camels and went back with the man. So the servant took Rebekah and left.

Now Isaac had come from Beer Lahai Roi, for he was living in the Negev. He went out to the field one evening to meditate, and as he looked up, he saw camels approaching.

Rebekah also looked up and saw Isaac. She got down from her camel and asked the servant, "Who is that man in the field coming to meet us?"

"He is my master," the servant answered. So she took her veil and covered herself. Then the servant told Isaac all he had done.

Isaac brought her into the tent of his mother Sarah, and he married Rebekah.

So she became his wife, and he loved her; and Isaac was comforted after his mother's death.

Application

Reflect on how God's guidance has played a role in your own relationships, whether romantic, familial, or friendships.

Express gratitude for these blessings, and pray for continued guidance in your relationships.

Lord Teach Me To	I Am Thankful For

Prayer

Heavenly Father, thank You for Your divine guidance in bringing people into my life.

I am grateful for the relationships You have blessed me with, and I pray that You continue to guide me in fostering and nurturing these connections. **Amen.**

Day 6: Jacob and Esau

Reflection

The story of Jacob and Esau demonstrates the consequences of deceit and rivalry within a family.

Despite their differences and the conflict that arose between them, God used their story to fulfill His purpose for their descendants.

Reflect on the importance of reconciliation, forgiveness, and the role God plays in working through difficult family dynamics.

Bible Passage :   Genesis 25:19-26 (NIV)

This is the account of the family line of Abraham's son Isaac. Abraham became the father of Isaac, and Isaac was forty years old when he married Rebekah daughter of Bethuel the Aramean from Paddan Aram and sister of Laban the Aramean. Isaac prayed to the LORD on behalf of his wife, because she was childless.

The LORD answered his prayer, and his wife Rebekah became pregnant. The babies jostled each other within her, and she said, "Why is this happening to me?" So she went to inquire of the LORD.

The LORD said to her, "Two nations are in your womb, and two peoples from within you will be separated; one people will be stronger than the other, and the older will serve the younger." When the time came for her to give birth, there were twin boys in her womb.

The first to come out was red, and his whole body was like a hairy garment; so they named him Esau. After this, his brother came out, with his hand grasping Esau's heel; so he was named Jacob. Isaac was sixty years old when Rebekah gave birth to them.

Application

Reflect on any unresolved conflicts or strained relationships within your own family.

Consider how you can work towards reconciliation, forgiveness, and healing. Pray for God's guidance in resolving these issues.

Lord Teach Me To	I Am Thankful For

Prayer

Lord, I ask for Your guidance and wisdom in dealing with difficult family dynamics.

Help me to work towards forgiveness, reconciliation, and healing in my relationships. **Amen.**

Day 7: Joseph's Dreams

Reflection

Joseph's story is a powerful example of how God can use the most challenging circumstances for His purposes.

Despite the jealousy and betrayal he faced from his brothers, Joseph's dreams and unwavering faith led him on a journey that ultimately brought him to a position of power and influence.

Reflect on how God has worked in your life during difficult times, using those situations to bring about His greater plan.

Bible Passage : Genesis 37:3-11 (NIV)

Now Israel loved Joseph more than any of his other sons, because he had been born to him in his old age; and he made an ornate robe for him. When his brothers saw that their father loved him more than any of them, they hated him and could not speak a kind word to him.
Joseph had a dream, and when he told it to his brothers, they hated him all the more. He said to them, "Listen to this dream I had:

We were binding sheaves of grain out in the field when suddenly my sheaf rose and stood upright, while your sheaves gathered around mine and bowed down to it." His brothers said to him, "Do you intend to reign over us? Will you actually rule us?" And they hated him all the more because of his dream and what he had said.Then he had another dream, and he told it to his brothers. "Listen," he said, "I had another dream, and this time the sun and moon and eleven stars were bowing down to me."

When he told his father as well as his brothers, his father rebuked him and said, "What is this dream you had? Will your mother and I and your brothers actually come and bow down to the ground before you?"
His brothers were jealous of him, but his father kept the matter in mind.

Application

Think about a challenging situation you have faced in the past.

Reflect on how God may have used that situation to guide you to a new opportunity or to help you grow in your faith. Pray for the ability to trust in God's plan, even when facing adversity.

Lord Teach Me To	**I Am Thankful For**

Prayer

Lord, help me to trust in Your plan and guidance, even when I face difficult circumstances.

Teach me to see Your hand at work in my life and to recognize the ways in which You use adversity for my growth and Your purposes. **Amen.**

Day 8: Moses and the Burning Bush

Reflection

The story of Moses and the burning bush highlights God's power and His ability to call ordinary people to do extraordinary things.

Moses, despite his initial doubts and feelings of inadequacy, answered God's call and became a great leader who delivered the Israelites from slavery in Egypt.

Reflect on times when you may have felt inadequate or unprepared for a task, and consider how God may be calling you to trust in His power and guidance.

Bible Passage :   Exodus 3:1-6 (NIV)

Now Moses was tending the flock of Jethro his father-in-law, the priest of Midian, and he led the flock to the far side of the wilderness and came to Horeb, the mountain of God. There the angel of the LORD appeared to him in flames of fire from within a bush. Moses saw that though the bush was on fire it did not burn up.

So Moses thought, "I will go over and see this strange sight—why the bush does not burn up." When the LORD saw that he had gone over to look, God called to him from within the bush, "Moses! Moses!" And Moses said, "Here I am."

"Do not come any closer," God said. "Take off your sandals, for the place where you are standing is holy ground."
Then he said, "I am the God of your father, the God of Abraham, the God of Isaac and the God of Jacob." At this, Moses hid his face, because he was afraid to look at God.

Application

Contemplate a situation in which you felt God calling you to do something beyond your comfort zone or abilities.

Reflect on how relying on God's strength and guidance helped you overcome any doubts or fears.

Pray for the courage to answer God's call, even when it seems daunting.

Lord Teach Me To	I Am Thankful For

Prayer

Heavenly Father, thank You for calling me to serve You in ways I may never have imagined.

Help me to trust in Your strength and guidance, even when I feel inadequate or unprepared. Give me the courage to step out in faith and answer Your call. **Amen.**

Day 9: The Ten Plagues

Reflection

The story of the ten plagues demonstrates God's power and His commitment to deliver His people from oppression.

As you read about each of the plagues, consider how they not only brought judgment upon the Egyptians but also affirmed the faith of the Israelites in the one true God.

Reflect on how God has shown His power and faithfulness in your own life.

Bible Passage : Exodus 7:14-25; 8; 9; 10; 11:1-10 (NIV)

Then the LORD said to Moses, "Pharaoh's heart is unyielding; he refuses to let the people go. Go to Pharaoh in the morning as he goes out to the river. Confront him on the bank of the Nile, and take in your hand the staff that was changed into a snake.

Then say to him, 'The LORD, the God of the Hebrews, has sent me to say to you: Let my people go, so that they may worship me in the wilderness. But until now you have not listened.'"

Highlights of the Ten Plagues:
Water turned to blood (Exodus 7:14-25)
Frogs (Exodus 8:1-15)
Gnats (Exodus 8:16-19)
Flies (Exodus 8:20-32)
Livestock diseased (Exodus 9:1-7)
Boils (Exodus 9:8-12)
Hail (Exodus 9:13-35)
Locusts (Exodus 10:1-20)
Darkness (Exodus 10:21-29)
Death of the firstborn (Exodus 11:1-10)

Application

Reflect on a time when you witnessed God's power and faithfulness in your life or the lives of others. Consider how these experiences have strengthened your faith and trust in God.

Pray for a deeper understanding of God's power and His desire to work in your life.

Lord Teach Me To	I Am Thankful For

Prayer

Lord, I am in awe of Your power and faithfulness. Thank You for the countless ways You have demonstrated Your love and commitment to Your people throughout history.

Help me to trust in Your power and to rely on You in all circumstances. **Amen.**

Day 10: The Exodus and the Red Sea

Reflection

The Exodus and the parting of the Red Sea are some of the most remarkable events in the Bible. These events not only demonstrate God's power but also His faithfulness to deliver His people. As you read about the Israelites' journey, consider how God's guidance and protection are still present in your own life. Reflect on times when you have experienced God's deliverance and provision.

Bible Passage :   Exodus 14:10-31 (NIV)

As Pharaoh approached, the Israelites looked up, and there were the Egyptians, marching after them. They were terrified and cried out to the LORD. 11 They said to Moses, "Was it because there were no graves in Egypt that you brought us to the desert to die? What have you done to us by bringing us out of Egypt? Didn't we say to you in Egypt, 'Leave us alone; let us serve the Egyptians'?

It would have been better for us to serve the Egyptians than to die in the desert!" Moses answered the people, "Do not be afraid. Stand firm and you will see the deliverance the LORD will bring you today.

The Egyptians you see today you will never see again. The LORD will fight for you; you need only to be still." Then the LORD said to Moses, "Why are you crying out to me? Tell the Israelites to move on. Raise your staff and stretch out your hand over the sea to divide the water so that the Israelites can go through the sea on dry ground. I will harden the hearts of the Egyptians so that they will go in after them. And I will gain glory through Pharaoh and all his army, through his chariots and his horsemen.

The Egyptians will know that I am the LORD when I gain glory through Pharaoh, his chariots and his horsemen."

Then the angel of God, who had been traveling in front of Israel's army, withdrew and went behind them. The pillar of cloud also moved from in front and stood behind them, 20 coming between the armies of Egypt and Israel. Throughout the night the cloud brought darkness to the one side and light to the other side; so neither went near the other all night long.

Then Moses stretched out his hand over the sea, and all that night the Lord drove the sea back with a strong east wind and turned it into dry land. The waters were divided, and the Israelites went through the sea on dry ground, with a wall of water on their right and on their left.

The Egyptians pursued them, and all Pharaoh's horses and chariots and horsemen followed them into the sea. During the last watch of the night the Lord looked down from the pillar of fire and cloud at the Egyptian army and threw it into confusion. He jammed the wheels of their chariots so that they had difficulty driving. And the Egyptians said, "Let's get away from the Israelites! The Lord is fighting for them against Egypt."

Then the Lord said to Moses, "Stretch out your hand over the sea so that the waters may flow back over the Egyptians and their chariots and horsemen." Moses stretched out his hand over the sea, and at daybreak the sea went back to its place. The Egyptians were fleeing toward it, and the Lord swept them into the sea. The water flowed back and covered the chariots and horsemen—the entire army of Pharaoh that had followed the Israelites into the sea. Not one of them survived. But the Israelites went through the sea on dry ground, with a wall of water on their right and on their left. That day the Lord saved Israel from the hands of the Egyptians, and Israel saw the Egyptians lying dead on the shore. And when the Israelites saw the mighty hand of the LORD displayed against the Egyptians, the people feared the LORD and put their trust in him and in Moses his servant.

Application

Recall a time when you faced a seemingly insurmountable challenge or obstacle. Reflect on how God provided for you or opened a way when it seemed impossible.
Pray for the faith to trust in God's deliverance and provision, even in the most difficult circumstances.

Prayer

Heavenly Father, thank You for Your faithfulness in delivering Your people and providing for their needs. Help me to trust in Your guidance and protection, even when faced with challenges that seem impossible to overcome. Increase my faith and dependence on You in all areas of my life **Amen.**

Day 11: The Ten Commandments

Reflection

The Ten Commandments are a foundational part of God's covenant with His people, providing a blueprint for a healthy and flourishing relationship with both God and others. As you read through the commandments, consider how they continue to shape our understanding of right and wrong, and reflect on the importance of living a life that honors God and respects others.

Bible Passage : Exodus 20:1-15 (NIV)

And God spoke all these words:
I am the LORD your God, who brought you out of Egypt, out of the land of slavery. "You shall have no other gods before me. You shall not make for yourself an idol in the form of anything in heaven above or on the earth beneath or in the waters below.

You shall not bow down to them or worship them; for I, the LORD your God, am a jealous God, punishing the children for the sin of the parents to the third and fourth generation of those who hate me, but showing love to a thousand generations of those who love me and keep my commandments.

You shall not misuse the name of the LORD your God, for the LORD will not hold anyone guiltless who misuses his name. Remember the Sabbath day by keeping it holy. Six days you shall labor and do all your work, but the seventh day is a sabbath to the LORD your God. On it you shall not do any work, neither you, nor your son or daughter, nor your male or female servant, nor your animals, nor any foreigner residing in your towns.

For in six days the LORD made the heavens and the earth, the sea, and all that is in them, but he rested on the seventh day. Therefore the LORD blessed the Sabbath day and made it holy. Honor your father and your mother, so that you may live long in the land the LORD your God is giving you.
You shall not murder.
You shall not commit adultery.
You shall not steal.
You shall not give false testimony against your neighbor.
You shall not covet your neighbor's house.
You shall not covet your neighbor's wife, or his male or female servant, his ox or donkey, or anything that belongs to your neighbor."

Application

Examine your own life in light of the Ten Commandments. Are there areas where you struggle to live up to these principles?

Pray for God's grace and guidance in helping you to follow His commandments and to grow in your relationship with Him and others.

Lord Teach Me To	**I Am Thankful For**

Prayer

Lord, thank You for the Ten Commandments and for providing us with a framework for living in harmony with You and others.

Help me to grow in my understanding of Your commandments and to apply them in my daily life. Grant me the wisdom and strength to honor You and respect those around me. **Amen.**

Day 12: The Promised Land

Reflection

The story of the Israelites' journey to the Promised Land is one of faith, perseverance, and God's faithfulness.

Despite the challenges and setbacks they faced, God remained with them, guiding them towards the land He had promised.

As you read about the Israelites' journey, reflect on your own spiritual journey and the ways in which God has been faithful to you.

Bible Passage :   Joshua 1:1-9 (NIV)

After the death of Moses the servant of the LORD, the LORD said to Joshua son of Nun, Moses' aide: Moses my servant is dead. Now then, you and all these people, get ready to cross the Jordan River into the land I am about to give to them—to the Israelites.

I will give you every place where you set your foot, as I promised Moses. Your territory will extend from the desert to Lebanon, and from the great river, the Euphrates—all the Hittite country—to the Mediterranean Sea in the west. No one will be able to stand against you all the days of your life. As I was with Moses, so I will be with you; I will never leave you nor forsake you.

Be strong and courageous, because you will lead these people to inherit the land I swore to their ancestors to give them. Be strong and very courageous. Be careful to obey all the law my servant Moses gave you; do not turn from it to the right or to the left, that you may be successful wherever you go.

Keep this Book of the Law always on your lips; meditate on it day and night, so that you may be careful to do everything written in it. Then you will be prosperous and successful. Have I not commanded you? Be strong and courageous. Do not be afraid; do not be discouraged, for the LORD your God will be with you wherever you go.

Application

Reflect on your own spiritual journey and the ways in which God has guided and provided for you. Are there areas in your life where you need to trust God more fully?

Pray for the strength and courage to follow God's leading, even when faced with challenges and

Lord Teach Me To	I Am Thankful For

Prayer

Heavenly Father, thank You for Your faithfulness and guidance in my life.

Help me to trust in Your promises and to follow Your leading with courage and perseverance. Grant me the strength to face challenges and uncertainties, knowing that You are with me wherever I go. **Amen.**

Day 13: Gideon's Victory

Reflection

The story of Gideon's victory over the Midianites is a testament to God's power and faithfulness, as well as a reminder that He can use ordinary people to achieve extraordinary things.

As you read Gideon's story, consider how God has equipped and empowered you for His purposes, even in the face of overwhelming odds.

Bible Passage : Judges 7:1-22 (NIV)

Early in the morning, Jerub-Baal (that is, Gideon) and all his men camped at the spring of Harod. The camp of Midian was north of them in the valley near the hill of Moreh. The LORD said to Gideon, "You have too many men. I cannot deliver Midian into their hands, or Israel would boast against me, 'My own strength has saved me.'

Now announce to the army, 'Anyone who trembles with fear may turn back and leave Mount Gilead.'" So twenty-two thousand men left, while ten thousand remained. But the Lord said to Gideon, "There are still too many men. Take them down to the water, and I will thin them out for you there. If I say, 'This one shall go with you,' he shall go; but if I say, 'This one shall not go with you,' he shall not go." So Gideon took the men down to the water. There the Lord told him, "Separate those who lap the water with their tongues as a dog laps from those who kneel down to drink." Three hundred of them drank from cupped hands, lapping like dogs. All the rest got down on their knees to drink.

The Lord said to Gideon, "With the three hundred men that lapped I will save you and give the Midianites into your hands. Let all the others go home." So Gideon sent the rest of the Israelites home but kept the three hundred, who took over the provisions and trumpets of the others.

Now the camp of Midian lay below him in the valley. During that night the Lord said to Gideon, "Get up, go down against the camp, because I am going to give it into your hands. If you are afraid to attack, go down to the camp with your servant Purah and listen to what they are saying. Afterward, you will be encouraged to attack the camp." So he and Purah his servant went down to the outposts of the camp.

The Midianites, the Amalekites and all the other eastern peoples had settled in the valley, thick as locusts. Their camels could no more be counted than the sand on the seashore.

Gideon arrived just as a man was telling a friend his dream. "I had a dream," he was saying. "A round loaf of barley bread came tumbling into the Midianite camp. It struck the tent with such force that the tent overturned and collapsed."
His friend responded, "This can be nothing other than the sword of Gideon son of Joash, the Israelite. God has given the Midianites and the whole camp into his hands." When Gideon heard the dream and its interpretation, he bowed down and worshiped. He returned to the camp of Israel and called out, "Get up! The Lord has given the Midianite camp into your hands." Dividing the three hundred men into three companies, he placed trumpets and empty jars in the hands of all of them, with torches inside.

"Watch me," he told them. "Follow my lead. When I get to the edge of the camp, do exactly as I do. When I and all who are with me blow our trumpets, then from all around the camp blow yours and shout, 'For the Lord and for Gideon.'"

Gideon and the hundred men with him reached the edge of the camp at the beginning of the middle watch, just after they had changed the guard. They blew their trumpets and broke the jars that were in their hands.
The three companies blew the trumpets and smashed the jars. Grasping the torches in their left hands and holding in their right hands the trumpets they were to blow, they shouted, "A sword for the Lord and for Gideon!"
While each man held his position around the camp, all the Midianites ran, crying out as they fled. When the three hundred trumpets sounded, the LORD caused the men throughout the camp to turn on each other with their swords. The army fled to Beth Shittah toward Zererah as far as the border of Abel Meholah near Tabbath.

Application

Reflect on the ways God has used you or someone you know, despite seemingly insurmountable odds or personal limitations. How can you trust God to use your gifts, talents, and circumstances for His purposes? Pray for the courage to step out in faith and to trust in God's guidance and provision.

Prayer

Lord, thank You for the story of Gideon and for the reminder that You can use ordinary people to accomplish extraordinary things. Help me to trust in Your power and provision, and to be open to Your leading in my life. Give me the courage to step out in faith, knowing that You are with me every step of the way. **Amen.**

Day 14: Samson's Strength

Reflection

The story of Samson is a cautionary tale of great strength and potential squandered due to poor choices and a lack of self-control.

As you read about Samson's life, consider how you can learn from his mistakes and use your God-given gifts and abilities for His glory, rather than your own.

Bible Passage : Judges 16:23-30 (NIV)

Now the rulers of the Philistines assembled to offer a great sacrifice to Dagon their god and to celebrate, saying, "Our god has delivered Samson, our enemy, into our hands." When the people saw him, they praised their god, saying, "Our god has delivered our enemy into our hands, the one who laid waste our land and multiplied our slain."

While they were in high spirits, they shouted, "Bring out Samson to entertain us." So they called Samson out of the prison, and he performed for them. When they stood him among the pillars,
Samson said to the servant who held his hand, "Put me where I can feel the pillars that support the temple, so that I may lean against them."
Now the temple was crowded with men and women; all the rulers of the Philistines were there, and on the roof were about three thousand men and women watching Samson perform.

Then Samson prayed to the LORD, "Sovereign LORD, remember me. Please, God, strengthen me just once more, and let me with one blow get revenge on the Philistines for my two eyes."
Then Samson reached toward the two central pillars on which the temple stood. Bracing himself against them, his right hand on the one and his left hand on the other,

Samson said, "Let me die with the Philistines!" Then he pushed with all his might, and down came the temple on the rulers and all the people in it. Thus he killed many more when he died than while he lived.

Application

Reflect on the lessons to be learned from Samson's life. How can you use your God-given gifts and abilities for His purposes, rather than seeking personal glory or satisfaction?

Pray for the wisdom and self-control to make choices that honor God and align with His will for your life.

Lord Teach Me To	I Am Thankful For

Prayer

Lord, thank You for the story of Samson and the lessons it teaches about the importance of using our gifts and abilities for Your glory.

Help me to learn from Samson's mistakes and to seek Your guidance and wisdom in all that I do. Grant me the self-control and discernment to make choices that honor You and further Your kingdom. **Amen.**

Day 15: Ruth's Loyalty

Reflection

The story of Ruth is a powerful example of loyalty, love, and faithfulness.

As you read about Ruth's devotion to her mother-in-law, Naomi, and her commitment to God, consider how you can demonstrate similar qualities in your own relationships and faith journey.

Bible Passage : Ruth 1:16-17 (NIV)

But Ruth replied, "Don't urge me to leave you or to turn back from you. Where you go I will go, and where you stay I will stay. Your people will be my people and your God my God.

Where you die I will die, and there I will be buried. May the LORD deal with me, be it ever so severely, if even death separates you and me."

Application

Reflect on the qualities that Ruth displayed in her relationship with Naomi, and how they can be applied to your own life.

How can you demonstrate loyalty, love, and faithfulness to God and the people in your life? Pray for the strength and wisdom to grow in these qualities and to be a blessing to others.

Lord Teach Me To	I Am Thankful For

Prayer

Lord, thank You for the story of Ruth and her inspiring example of loyalty, love, and faithfulness. Help me to grow in these qualities and to demonstrate them in my relationships with others and in my walk with You.

Grant me the strength and wisdom to be a blessing to those around me, just as Ruth was to Naomi. **Amen.**

Day 16: The Anointing of King David

Reflection

The anointing of David as king demonstrates God's ability to see beyond appearances and choose those who have a heart for Him. As you read about David's anointing, consider how God has chosen you for specific purposes and how you can cultivate a heart that is pleasing to Him.

Bible Passage : 1 Samuel 16:1-13 (NIV)

The LORD said to Samuel, "How long will you mourn for Saul, since I have rejected him as king over Israel? Fill your horn with oil and be on your way; I am sending you to Jesse of Bethlehem. I have chosen one of his sons to be king."

But Samuel said, "How can I go? If Saul hears about it, he will kill me." The LORD said, "Take a heifer with you and say, 'I have come to sacrifice to the LORD.' Invite Jesse to the sacrifice, and I will show you what to do. You are to anoint for me the one I indicate."

Samuel did what the LORD said. When he arrived at Bethlehem, the elders of the town trembled when they met him. They asked, "Do you come in peace?" Samuel replied, "Yes, in peace; I have come to sacrifice to the LORD. Consecrate yourselves and come to the sacrifice with me." Then he consecrated Jesse and his sons and invited them to the sacrifice. When they arrived, Samuel saw Eliab and thought, "Surely the LORD's anointed stands here before the LORD."

But the LORD said to Samuel, "Do not consider his appearance or his height, for I have rejected him. The LORD does not look at the things people look at. People look at the outward appearance, but the LORD looks at the heart."
Then Jesse called Abinadab and had him pass in front of Samuel. But Samuel said, "The LORD has not chosen this one either." Jesse then had Shammah pass by, but Samuel said, "Nor has the LORD chosen this one." Jesse had seven of his sons pass before Samuel, but Samuel said to him, "The LORD has not chosen these." So he asked Jesse, "Are these all the sons you have?"

"There is still the youngest," Jesse answered. "He is tending the sheep." Samuel said, "Send for So he sent for him and had him brought in. He was glowing with health and had a fine appearance and handsome features. Then the LORD said, "Rise and anoint him; this is the one." So Samuel took the horn of oil and anointed him in the presence of his brothers, and from that day on the Spirit of the LORD came powerfully upon David. Samuel then went to Ramah.

Application

Reflect on how God has chosen you for specific purposes in your life.

How can you cultivate a heart that is pleasing to Him and focus on developing godly character? Pray for the wisdom and discernment to recognize and fulfill the purposes God has for you.

Lord Teach Me To	**I Am Thankful For**

Prayer

Heavenly Father, thank You for the story of David's anointing and the reminder that You look at the heart, not outward appearances.

Help me to cultivate a heart that is pleasing to You and to focus on developing godly character. Grant me the wisdom and discernment to recognize and fulfill the purposes You have for me. **Amen.**

Day 17: David and Goliath

Reflection

The story of David and Goliath is an inspiring tale of courage, faith, and trusting in God's power.

As you read about David's triumph over the giant, consider the "giants" you face in your own life and how trusting in God can help you overcome them.

Bible Passage : 1 Samuel 17:45-50 (NIV)

David said to the Philistine, "You come against me with sword and spear and javelin, but I come against you in the name of the LORD Almighty, the God of the armies of Israel, whom you have defied.

This day the LORD will deliver you into my hands, and I'll strike you down and cut off your head. This very day I will give the carcasses of the Philistine army to the birds and the wild animals, and the whole world will know that there is a God in Israel.

All those gathered here will know that it is not by sword or spear that the LORD saves; for the battle is the LORD's, and he will give all of you into our hands."

As the Philistine moved closer to attack him, David ran quickly toward the battle line to meet him.

Reaching into his bag and taking out a stone, he slung it and struck the Philistine on the forehead. The stone sank into his forehead, and he fell facedown on the ground.

So David triumphed over the Philistine with a sling and a stone; without a sword in his hand he struck down the Philistine and
killed him.

Application

Reflect on the story of David and Goliath and how it relates to your own life. What "giants" are you facing? How can you trust in God's power to help you overcome these challenges?

Pray for the faith and courage to face your giants, and for the wisdom to rely on God's strength rather than your own.

Lord Teach Me To	I Am Thankful For

Prayer

Heavenly Father, thank You for the inspiring story of David and Goliath. Help me to face the "giants" in my life with courage and faith, trusting in Your power to overcome them.

Grant me the wisdom to rely on Your strength and not my own, and to recognize that the battle is Yours. **Amen.**

Day 18: Solomon's Wisdom

Reflection

The story of Solomon's wisdom highlights the importance of seeking God's wisdom above all else.

As you read about Solomon's request for wisdom and how it impacted his reign, consider the areas of your life where you need God's wisdom and guidance.

Bible Passage : 1 Kings 3:5-12 (NIV)

At Gibeon the LORD appeared to Solomon during the night in a dream, and God said, "Ask for whatever you want me to give you."

Solomon answered, "You have shown great kindness to your servant, my father David, because he was faithful to you and righteous and upright in heart. You have continued this great kindness to him and have given him a son to sit on his throne this very day.

Now, LORD my God, you have made your servant king in place of my father David. But I am only a little child and do not know how to carry out my duties.Your servant is here among the people you have chosen, a great people, too numerous to count or number.

So give your servant a discerning heart to govern your people and to distinguish between right and wrong. For who is able to govern this great people of yours?"

The Lord was pleased that Solomon had asked for this.

So God said to him, "Since you have asked for this and not for long life or wealth for yourself, nor have asked for the death of your enemies but for discernment in administering justice,

I will do what you have asked. I will give you a wise and discerning heart, so that there will never have been anyone like you, nor will there ever be."

Application

Reflect on the story of Solomon and how it demonstrates the importance of seeking God's wisdom. In what areas of your life do you need God's wisdom and guidance?

Pray for a discerning heart and the humility to seek God's wisdom above all else.

Lord Teach Me To	I Am Thankful For

Prayer

Lord, thank You for the story of Solomon and the example it sets for seeking Your wisdom.

Help me to recognize my need for Your guidance and to humbly seek Your wisdom in all areas of my life. Grant me a discerning heart and the willingness to follow Your leading. **Amen.**

Day 19: Elijah and the Prophets of Baal

Reflection

The story of Elijah and the Prophets of Baal is a powerful testimony to God's sovereignty and power.

As you read about Elijah's challenge to the prophets of the false god Baal, consider the ways in which you can stand strong in your faith and trust in God's power, even when facing opposition.

Bible Passage : 1 Kings 18:36-39 (NIV)

At the time of sacrifice, the prophet Elijah stepped forward and prayed: "LORD, the God of Abraham, Isaac and Israel, let it be known today that you are God in Israel and that I am your servant and have done all these things at your command.

Answer me, LORD, answer me, so these people will know that you, LORD, are God, and that you are turning their hearts back again."

Then the fire of the LORD fell and burned up the sacrifice, the wood, the stones and the soil, and also licked up the water in the trench.

When all the people saw this, they fell prostrate and cried, "The LORD——he is God! The LORD—he is God!"

Application

Reflect on the story of Elijah and the Prophets of Baal, and how it demonstrates God's power and sovereignty. How can you stand strong in your faith and trust in God's power, even when facing opposition or doubt?

Pray for the courage and conviction to remain steadfast in your faith, and for the wisdom to recognize God's hand at work in your life.

Lord Teach Me To	**I Am Thankful For**

Prayer

Heavenly Father, thank You for the story of Elijah and the powerful demonstration of Your sovereignty and power. Help me to stand strong in my faith, trusting in Your power even when facing opposition or doubt.

Grant me the courage and conviction to remain steadfast in my faith, and the wisdom to recognize Your hand at work in my life. **Amen.**

Day 20: Elisha's Miracles

Reflection

The story of Elisha's miracles showcases God's power and compassion in the lives of His people.

As you read about the many miracles performed by Elisha through God's power, consider how God continues to work in your life and the lives of those around you.

Bible Passage : 2 Kings 4:1-7 (NIV)

The wife of a man from the company of the prophets cried out to Elisha, "Your servant my husband is dead, and you know that he revered the LORD. But now his creditor is coming to take my two boys as his slaves."

Elisha replied to her, "How can I help you? Tell me, what do you have in your house?" "Your servant has nothing there at all," she said, "except a small jar of olive oil."

Elisha said, "Go around and ask all your neighbors for empty jars. Don't ask for just a few.

Then go inside and shut the door behind you and your sons. Pour oil into all the jars, and as each is filled, put it to one side."

She left him and shut the door behind her and her sons. They brought the jars to her, and she kept pouring.

When all the jars were full, she said to her son, "Bring me another one."

She went and told the man of God, and he said, "Go, sell the oil and pay your debts. You and your sons can live on what is left."

Application

Reflect on the story of Elisha's miracles and how they demonstrate God's power and compassion. In what ways have you experienced God's power and compassion in your life?

How can you share these experiences with others to encourage them in their faith? Pray for a heart that is open to recognizing God's work in your life, and for the boldness to share your testimony with others.

Lord Teach Me To	I Am Thankful For

Prayer

Lord, thank You for the stories of Elisha's miracles and the powerful reminders of Your power and compassion.

Help me to recognize Your work in my life and to share my experiences with others to encourage and strengthen their faith. Grant me a heart that is open to Your work, and the boldness to share my testimony. **Amen.**

Day 21: Jonah and the Great Fish

Reflection

The story of Jonah and the Great Fish is a reminder of God's mercy and His desire for all people to come to repentance.

As you read about Jonah's reluctance to follow God's command and his eventual submission, consider the areas of your life where you need to submit to God's will and trust in His plan.

Bible Passage : Jonah 1:17, 2:10, 3:1-5 (NIV)

Now the LORD provided a huge fish to swallow Jonah, and Jonah was in the belly of the fish three days and three nights.

And the LORD commanded the fish, and it vomited Jonah onto dry land.

Then the word of the LORD came to Jonah a second time:

"Go to the great city of Nineveh and proclaim to it the message I give you."

Jonah obeyed the word of the LORD and went to Nineveh. Now Nineveh was a very large city; it took three days to go through it.

Jonah began by going a day's journey into the city, proclaiming, "Forty more days and Nineveh will be overthrown."

The Ninevites believed God. A fast was proclaimed, and all of them, from the greatest to the least, put on sackcloth.

Application

Reflect on the story of Jonah and the Great Fish, and consider how it relates to your own life. In what areas do you need to submit to God's will and trust in His plan?

Pray for the humility to submit to God's leading and the willingness to follow His guidance, even when it's challenging.

Lord Teach Me To

I Am Thankful For

Prayer

Heavenly Father, thank You for the story of Jonah and the reminder of Your mercy and desire for all people to come to repentance. Help me to submit to Your will and trust in Your plan for my life, even when it's difficult.
Grant me the humility to follow Your guidance and the willingness to obey Your commands. **Amen.**

Day 22: Isaiah's Prophecies

Reflection

The prophecies of Isaiah serve as powerful reminders of God's sovereignty and faithfulness.

As you read about Isaiah's prophetic words concerning the coming Messiah and the future restoration of Israel, consider how God's promises continue to be fulfilled in your own life and the world around you.

Bible Passage : Isaiah 9:6-7 (NIV)

For to us a child is born, to us a son is given, and the government will be on his shoulders. And he will be called Wonderful Counselor, Mighty God, Everlasting Father, Prince of Peace.

Of the greatness of his government and peace there will be no end. He will reign on David's throne and over his kingdom, establishing and upholding it with justice and righteousness from that time on and forever. The zeal of the LORD Almighty will accomplish this.

Application

Reflect on the prophecies of Isaiah and their significance in your faith journey. How have you seen God's promises fulfilled in your life and the world around you?

Pray for a deeper understanding of God's sovereignty and faithfulness, and for the ability to trust in His promises even when faced with challenges and uncertainties.

Lord Teach Me To	I Am Thankful For

Prayer

Lord, thank You for the prophecies of Isaiah and the reminders of Your sovereignty and faithfulness. Help me to see Your promises being fulfilled in my life and the world around me. Grant me a deeper understanding of

Your faithfulness, and help me trust in Your promises even when faced with challenges and uncertainties. **Amen.**

Day 23: Daniel in the Lion's Den

Reflection

The story of Daniel in the Lion's Den demonstrates the power of faith and trust in God, even when faced with seemingly insurmountable obstacles.

As you read about Daniel's unwavering commitment to prayer and his miraculous deliverance from the lions, consider how you can deepen your own faith and trust in God.

Bible Passage :   Daniel 6:10, 16, 22-23 (NIV)

Now when Daniel learned that the decree had been published, he went home to his upstairs room where the windows opened toward Jerusalem. Three times a day he got down on his knees and prayed, giving thanks to his God, just as he had done before.

So the king gave the order, and they brought Daniel and threw him into the lions' den. The king said to Daniel, "May your God, whom you serve continually, rescue you!"

My God sent his angel, and he shut the mouths of the lions. They have not hurt me, because I was found innocent in his sight. Nor have I ever done any wrong before you, Your Majesty.

The king was overjoyed and gave orders to lift Daniel out of the den. And when Daniel was lifted from the den, no wound was found on him, because he had trusted in his God.

Application

Reflect on the story of Daniel in the Lion's Den and the power of faith and trust in God. How can you deepen your own faith and trust in God, even when faced with challenges or obstacles?

Pray for the courage and strength to maintain your faith, and for the wisdom to seek God's guidance in all aspects of your life.

Lord Teach Me To	I Am Thankful For

Prayer

Heavenly Father, thank You for the inspiring story of Daniel in the Lion's Den and the powerful example of faith and trust in You.

Help me to deepen my own faith and trust in You, even when faced with challenges or obstacles. Grant me the courage and strength to maintain my faith, and the wisdom to seek Your guidance in all aspects of my life. **Amen.**

Day 24: The Birth of Jesus

Reflection

The birth of Jesus marks the fulfillment of God's promise of a Savior and serves as a testament to His great love for humanity.

As you read the account of Jesus' humble birth, consider the depth of God's love for you and the incredible gift of salvation through His Son.

Bible Passage : Luke 2:6-14 (NIV)

While they were there, the time came for the baby to be born, and she gave birth to her firstborn, a son. She wrapped him in cloths and placed him in a manger, because there was no guest room available for them.

And there were shepherds living out in the fields nearby, keeping watch over their flocks at night.

An angel of the Lord appeared to them, and the glory of the Lord shone around them, and they were terrified.

But the angel said to them, "Do not be afraid. I bring you good news that will cause great joy for all the people.

Today in the town of David a Savior has been born to you; he is the Messiah, the Lord.

This will be a sign to you: You will find a baby wrapped in cloths and lying in a manger."

Suddenly a great company of the heavenly host appeared with the angel, praising God and saying,

"Glory to God in the highest heaven, and on earth peace to those on whom his favor rests."

Application

Reflect on the birth of Jesus and the incredible gift of salvation that His birth represents. How does the account of Jesus' birth deepen your understanding of God's love for you and His desire to redeem humanity?

Pray for a renewed sense of gratitude for the gift of salvation and for the ability to share this good news with others.

Lord Teach Me To	**I Am Thankful For**

Prayer

Lord, thank You for the incredible gift of Jesus' birth and the salvation it represents. Help me to understand more deeply the magnitude of Your love for me and Your desire to redeem humanity.

Fill my heart with gratitude for the gift of salvation, and give me the ability to share this good news with others. **Amen.**

Day 25: Jesus' Baptism and Temptation

Reflection

The account of Jesus' baptism and temptation provides important insights into His humanity and the spiritual battles that we all face. As you read about Jesus' submission to baptism and His resistance to temptation, consider the ways in which you can follow His example in your own spiritual journey.

Bible Passage : Matthew 3:13-17, 4:1-11 (NIV)

Then Jesus came from Galilee to the Jordan to be baptized by John.
But John tried to deter him, saying, "I need to be baptized by you, and do you come to me?"

Jesus replied, "Let it be so now; it is proper for us to do this to fulfill all righteousness." Then John consented. As soon as Jesus was baptized, he went up out of the water.
At that moment heaven was opened, and he saw the Spirit of God descending like a dove and alighting on him. And a voice from heaven said, "This is my Son, whom I love; with him I am well pleased."

Then Jesus was led by the Spirit into the wilderness to be tempted by the devil. After fasting forty days and forty nights, he was hungry. The tempter came to him and said, "If you are the Son of God, tell these stones to become bread."

Jesus answered, "It is written: 'Man shall not live on bread alone, but on every word that comes from the mouth of God.'"

Then the devil took him to the holy city and had him stand on the highest point of the temple. "If you are the Son of God," he said, "throw yourself down. For it is written: 'He will command his angels concerning you, and they will lift you up in their hands, so that you will not strike your foot against a stone.'"

Jesus answered him, "It is also written: 'Do not put the Lord your God to the test.'" Again, the devil took him to a very high mountain and showed him all the kingdoms of the world and their splendor.

"All this I will give you," he said, "if you will bow down and worship me."
Jesus said to him, "Away from me, Satan! For it is written: 'Worship the Lord
Then the devil left him, and angels came and attended him.

Application

Reflect on Jesus' baptism and temptation and how they relate to your own spiritual journey. How can you follow Jesus' example of submission to baptism and resistance to temptation?

Pray for the strength to resist temptation and for the humility to submit to God's will in all aspects of your life.

Lord Teach Me To	I Am Thankful For

Prayer

Heavenly Father, thank You for the example of Jesus' baptism and temptation.

Help me to follow His example of submission to Your will and resistance to temptation. Grant me the strength to resist the temptations I face and the humility to submit to Your will in all aspects of my life. **Amen.**

Day 26: The Sermon on the Mount

Reflection

The Sermon on the Mount, found in the Gospel of Matthew, is a collection of Jesus' teachings that provide a blueprint for living a godly life.
As you read and reflect on these teachings, consider how they can be applied to your own life and how they can guide your daily actions and decisions.

Bible Passage : Matthew 5:1-12, 7:24-27 (NIV)

Now when Jesus saw the crowds, he went up on a mountainside and sat down. His disciples came to him, and he began to teach them. He said:

Blessed are the poor in spirit, for theirs is the kingdom of heaven.
Blessed are those who mourn, for they will be comforted.
Blessed are the meek, for they will inherit the earth.
Blessed are those who hunger and thirst for righteousness, for they will be filled.
Blessed are the merciful, for they will be shown mercy.
Blessed are the pure in heart, for they will see God.
Blessed are the peacemakers, for they will be called children of God.
Blessed are those who are persecuted because of righteousness, for theirs is the kingdom of heaven.
Blessed are you when people insult you, persecute you and falsely say all kinds of evil against you because of me.

Rejoice and be glad, because great is your reward in heaven, for in the same way they persecuted the prophets who were before you."

Therefore everyone who hears these words of mine and puts them into practice is like a wise man who built his house on the rock. The rain came down, the streams rose, and the winds blew and beat against that house; yet it did not fall, because it had its foundation on the rock.

But everyone who hears these words of mine and does not put them into practice is like a foolish man who built his house on sand.
The rain came down, the streams rose, and the winds blew and beat against that house, and it fell with a great crash."

Application

Reflect on Jesus' teachings in the Sermon on the Mount and how they can guide your daily actions and decisions. Which of these teachings resonate most with you, and how can you apply them to your life?

Pray for the wisdom and strength to live out these teachings and to build your life upon the solid foundation of Jesus' words.

Lord Teach Me To	I Am Thankful For

Prayer

Lord Jesus, thank You for the guidance and wisdom found in the Sermon on the Mount. Help me to apply these teachings to my daily life and to build my life upon the solid foundation of Your words.

Grant me the wisdom and strength to live out these teachings and to be a shining example of Your love and grace. **Amen.**

Day 27: Jesus' Miracles and Teachings

Reflection

Throughout His ministry, Jesus performed many miracles and shared profound teachings that demonstrated His authority and power.
As you read about some of these miracles and teachings, consider the ways in which they reveal the nature of God and His kingdom.
Reflect on how these accounts can deepen your faith and understanding of who Jesus is.

Bible Passage : John 2:1-11 (NIV)

On the third day a wedding took place at Cana in Galilee. Jesus' mother was there, and Jesus and his disciples had also been invited to the wedding.

When the wine was gone, Jesus' mother said to him, "They have no more wine."

"Woman, why do you involve me?" Jesus replied. "My hour has not yet come." His mother said to the servants, "Do whatever he tells you."

Nearby stood six stone water jars, the kind used by the Jews for ceremonial washing, each holding from twenty to thirty gallons.

Jesus said to the servants, "Fill the jars with water"; so they filled them to the brim. Then he told them, "Now draw some out and take it to the master of the banquet."

They did so, and the master of the banquet tasted the water that had been turned into wine. He did not realize where it had come from, though the servants who had drawn the water knew. Then he called the bridegroom aside and said,

"Everyone brings out the choice wine first and then the cheaper wine after the guests have had too much to drink; but you have saved the best till now."

What Jesus did here in Cana of Galilee was the first of the signs through which he revealed his glory; and his disciples believed in him.

Bible Passage : Matthew 14:13-21 (NIV)

When Jesus heard what had happened, he withdrew by boat privately to a solitary place. Hearing of this, the crowds followed him on foot from the towns. When Jesus landed and saw a large crowd, he had compassion on them and healed their sick.

As evening approached, the disciples came to him and said, "This is a remote place, and it's already getting late. Send the crowds away, so they can go to the villages and buy themselves some food."
Jesus replied, "They do not need to go away. You give them something to eat." "We have here only five loaves of bread and two fish," they answered. "Bring them here to me," he said.

And he directed the people to sit down on the grass. Taking the five loaves and the two fish and looking up to heaven, he gave thanks and broke the loaves. Then he gave them to the disciples, and the disciples gave them to the people.

They all ate and were satisfied, and the disciples picked up twelve basketfuls of broken pieces that were left over. The number of those who ate was about five thousand men, besides women and children.

Application

Spend some time in nature today, observing the beauty and intricacy of God's creation.

Consider how you can be a better steward of the environment and the resources He has provided.

Prayer

Heavenly Father, thank You for the wonder and beauty of Your creation.

Help me to appreciate and care for the world You have made, and to recognize my place in Your grand design. **Amen.**

Day 28: The Parables of Jesus

Reflection

Parables are simple stories that Jesus used to convey profound spiritual truths. They reveal the mysteries of the kingdom of heaven in ways that are relatable and memorable. As you read and reflect on these parables, consider the spiritual lessons they offer and how you can apply them to your own life.

Bible Passage : Matthew 18:12-14; Luke 15:3-7 (NIV)

"What do you think? If a man owns a hundred sheep, and one of them wanders away, will he not leave the ninety-nine on the hills and go to look for the one that wandered off?
And if he finds it, truly I tell you, he is happier about that one sheep than about the ninety-nine that did not wander off. In the same way your Father in heaven is not willing that any of these little ones should perish.

Then Jesus told them this parable: "Suppose one of you has a hundred sheep and loses one of them. Doesn't he leave the ninety-nine in the open country and go after the lost sheep until he finds it?
And when he finds it, he joyfully puts it on his shoulders and goes home. Then he calls his friends and neighbors together and says, 'Rejoice with me; I have found my lost sheep.'

I tell you that in the same way there will be more rejoicing in heaven over one sinner who repents than over ninety-nine righteous persons who do not need to repent.

Bible Passage : Matthew 18:21-35 (NIV)

Then Peter came to Jesus and asked, "Lord, how many times shall I forgive my brother or sister who sins against me? Up to seven times?" Jesus answered, "I tell you, not seven times, but seventy-seven times.

"Therefore, the kingdom of heaven is like a king who wanted to settle accounts with his servants. As he began the settlement, a man who owed him ten thousand bags of gold was brought to him. Since he was not able to pay, the master ordered that he and his wife and his children and all that he had be sold to repay the debt.

"At this the servant fell on his knees before him. 'Be patient with me,' he begged, 'and I will pay back everything.' The servant's master took pity on him, canceled the debt and let him go.

"But when that servant went out, he found one of his fellow servants who owed him a hundred silver coins. He grabbed him and began to choke him. 'Pay back what you owe me!' he demanded.

"His fellow servant fell to his knees and begged him, 'Be patient with me, and I will pay it back.'

"But he refused. Instead, he went off and had the man thrown into prison until he could pay the debt. 31 When the other servants saw what had happened, they were outraged and went and told their master everything that had happened.

"Then the master called the servant in. 'You wicked servant,' he said, 'I canceled all that debt of yours because you begged me to. 33 Shouldn't you have had mercy on your fellow servant just as I had on you?' 34 In anger his master handed him over to the jailers to be tortured, until he should pay back all he owed.

"This is how my heavenly Father will treat each of you unless you forgive your brother or sister from your heart."

Application

Reflect on the parables of Jesus and the spiritual lessons they convey. Which of these parables resonate most with you, and how can you apply their lessons to your life? Pray for the wisdom and discernment to understand the deeper meanings of these parables and to allow them to transform your heart and mind.

Prayer

Lord Jesus, thank You for the wisdom and guidance found in Your parables. Help me to understand the deeper meanings of these stories and to apply their lessons to my daily life.
Grant me the wisdom and discernment to live out these teachings and to be a shining example of Your love and grace. **Amen.**

Day 29: The Transfiguration

Reflection

The Transfiguration of Jesus is a pivotal moment in the Gospels, as it demonstrates His divine nature and foreshadows His resurrection.

As you read and reflect on the Transfiguration, consider how this event strengthens your faith in Jesus as the Son of God and how it can inspire your spiritual journey.

Bible Passage :   Matthew 17:1-9 (NIV)

After six days Jesus took with him Peter, James and John the brother of James, and led them up a high mountain by themselves.

There he was transfigured before them. His face shone like the sun, and his clothes became as white as the light.

Just then there appeared before them Moses and Elijah, talking with Jesus.

Peter said to Jesus, "Lord, it is good for us to be here. If you wish, I will put up three shelters—one for you, one for Moses and one for Elijah."

While he was still speaking, a bright cloud covered them, and a voice from the cloud said, "This is my Son, whom I love; with him I am well pleased. Listen to him!"

When the disciples heard this, they fell facedown to the ground, terrified. But Jesus came and touched them. "Get up," he said. "Don't be afraid." When they looked up, they saw no one except Jesus.

As they were coming down the mountain, Jesus instructed them, "Don't tell anyone what you have seen, until the Son of Man has been raised from the dead."

Application

Reflect on the significance of the Transfiguration and how it affirms Jesus' divine nature. How does this event strengthen your faith in Jesus as the Son of God?

Pray for the grace to remain steadfast in your faith and to continually grow closer to Jesus in your spiritual journey.

Lord Teach Me To	I Am Thankful For

Prayer

Lord Jesus, thank You for revealing Your divine nature through the Transfiguration.
Strengthen my faith in You as the Son of God and help me to continually grow closer to You in my spiritual journey.
Grant me the grace to remain steadfast in my faith and to follow Your teachings and example. **Amen.**

Day 30: The Last Supper

Reflection

The Last Supper is a significant event in the Gospels, as it is the final meal Jesus shares with His disciples before His crucifixion. During this meal, Jesus establishes the Eucharist and demonstrates the importance of humility and service.

As you read and reflect on the Last Supper, consider how you can incorporate these lessons into your own life and relationships.

Bible Passage : Matthew 26:26-30

While they were eating, Jesus took bread, and when he had given thanks, he broke it and gave it to his disciples, saying, "Take and eat; this is my body."

Then he took a cup, and when he had given thanks, he gave it to them, saying, "Drink from it, all of you. This is my blood of the covenant, which is poured out for many for the forgiveness of sins. I tell you, I will not drink from this fruit of the vine from now on until that day when I drink it new with you in my Father's kingdom."

When they had sung a hymn, they went out to the Mount of Olives.

Bible Passage : John 13:1-17 (NIV)

It was just before the Passover Festival. Jesus knew that the hour had come for him to leave this world and go to the Father. Having loved his own who were in the world, he loved them to the end.

The evening meal was in progress, and the devil had already prompted Judas, the son of Simon Iscariot, to betray Jesus. Jesus knew that the Father had put all things under his power, and that he had come from God and was returning to God; so he got up from the meal, took off his outer clothing, and wrapped a towel around his waist. After that, he poured water into a basin and began to wash his disciples' feet, drying them with the towel that was wrapped around him.

He came to Simon Peter, who said to him, "Lord, are you going to wash my feet?"
Jesus replied, "You do not realize now what I am doing, but later you will understand." "No," said Peter, "you shall never wash my feet."
Jesus answered, "Unless I wash you, you have no part with me."
"Then, Lord," Simon Peter replied, "not just my feet but my hands and my head as well!"

Jesus answered, "Those who have had a bath need only to wash their feet; their whole body is clean. And you are clean, though not every one of you." For he knew who was going to betray him, and that was why he said not every one was clean.

When he had finished washing their feet, he put on his clothes and returned to his place. "Do you understand what I have done for you?" he asked them. "You call me 'Teacher' and 'Lord,' and rightly so, for that is what I am. Now that I, your Lord and Teacher, have washed your feet, you also should wash one another's feet. I have set you an example that you should do as I have done for you. Very truly I tell you, no servant is greater than his master, nor is a messenger greater than the one who sent him. Now that you know these things, you will be blessed if you do them."

Application

Reflect on the lessons of the Last Supper, including the significance of the Eucharist and Jesus' demonstration of humility and service.

Consider ways you can embody these qualities in your own life and relationships. How can you better serve those around you and exhibit a humble heart?

Prayer

Lord Jesus, thank You for the gift of the Last Supper, where You established the Eucharist and showed us the importance of humility and service. Help me to internalize these lessons and to be a reflection of Your love in my relationships with others. Guide me to serve those around me with a humble heart, following Your example, and to always remember the great sacrifice You made for us. **Amen.**

Day 31: The Crucifixion

Reflection

The Crucifixion is the most poignant and significant event in the life of Jesus. Through His death on the cross, Jesus paid the price for our sins and demonstrated His love for humanity.

As you read and reflect on the Crucifixion, contemplate the depth of Jesus' sacrifice and consider how it affects your life, your faith, and your relationship with God.

Bible Passage : Matthew 27:32-54 (NIV)

As they were going out, they met a man from Cyrene, named Simon, and they forced him to carry the cross. They came to a place called Golgotha (which means "the place of the skull"). There they offered Jesus wine to drink, mixed with gall; but after tasting it, he refused to drink it.

When they had crucified him, they divided up his clothes by casting lots. And sitting down, they kept watch over him there. Above his head they placed the written charge against him: THIS IS JESUS, THE KING OF THE JEWS.

Two rebels were crucified with him, one on his right and one on his left. Those who passed by hurled insults at him, shaking their heads and saying, "You who are going to destroy the temple and build it in three days, save yourself! Come down from the cross, if you are the Son of God!" In the same way the chief priests, the teachers of the law and the elders mocked him.

"He saved others," they said, "but he can't save himself! He's the king of Israel! Let him come down now from the cross, and we will believe in him. He trusts in God. Let God rescue him now if he wants him, for he said, 'I am the Son of God.'" In the same way the rebels who were crucified with him also heaped insults on him.

From noon until three in the afternoon darkness came over all the land. About three in the afternoon Jesus cried out in a loud voice, "Eli, Eli, lema sabachthani?" (which means "My God, my God, why have you forsaken me?").

When some of those standing there heard this, they said, "He's calling Elijah." Immediately one of them ran and got a sponge. He filled it with wine vinegar, put it on a staff, and offered it to Jesus to drink.

The rest said, "Now leave him alone. Let's see if Elijah comes to save him."

And when Jesus had cried out again in a loud voice, he gave up his spirit.

At that moment the curtain of the temple was torn in two from top to bottom. The earth shook, the rocks split and the tombs broke open. The bodies of many holy people who had died were raised to life.

They came out of the tombs after Jesus' resurrection and went into the holy city and appeared to many people.

When the centurion and those with him who were guarding Jesus saw the earthquake and all that had happened, they were terrified and exclaimed, "Surely he was the Son of God!"

Application

Reflect on the Crucifixion and the magnitude of Jesus' sacrifice for our sins. How does this event impact your life, your faith, and your relationship with God?

Consider the ways you can express gratitude for this sacrifice and live a life that honors Jesus' love and selflessness.

Prayer

Lord Jesus, thank You for the incredible sacrifice You made on the cross. Your love and selflessness are beyond measure, and I am forever grateful for the gift of salvation. Help me to live a life that honors Your sacrifice and to share Your love with others. Guide me in my faith journey, and remind me of the depth of Your love and forgiveness, even when I feel unworthy. Strengthen my resolve to follow You and to be a beacon of Your light in this world. In Your holy name, I pray. **Amen.**

Day 32: The Resurrection

Reflection

The Resurrection of Jesus is the cornerstone of the Christian faith. It is the ultimate demonstration of God's love and power, as Jesus triumphed over sin and death.

As you reflect on the Resurrection, consider the hope and assurance it brings to your own life and how it impacts your faith journey.

Bible Passage : John 20:1-18 (NIV)

Early on the first day of the week, while it was still dark, Mary Magdalene went to the tomb and saw that the stone had been removed from the entrance.
So she came running to Simon Peter and the other disciple, the one Jesus loved, and said, "They have taken the Lord out of the tomb, and we don't know where they have put him!" So Peter and the other disciple started for the tomb. Both were running, but the other disciple outran Peter and reached the tomb first. He bent over and looked in at the strips of linen lying there but did not go in.
Then Simon Peter came along behind him and went straight into the tomb. He saw the strips of linen lying there, as well as the cloth that had been wrapped around Jesus' head. The cloth was still lying in its place, separate from the linen. Finally, the other disciple, who had reached the tomb first, also went inside. He saw and believed. (They still did not understand from Scripture that Jesus had to rise from the dead.) Then the disciples went back to where they were staying.

Now Mary stood outside the tomb crying. As she wept, she bent over to look into the tomb and saw two angels in white, seated where Jesus' body had been, one at the head and the other at the foot.
They asked her, "Woman, why are you crying?" "They have taken my Lord away," she said, "and I don't know where they have put him."
At this, she turned around and saw Jesus standing there, but she did not realize that it was Jesus. He asked her, "Woman, why are you crying? Who is it you are looking for?" Thinking he was the gardener, she said, "Sir, if you have carried him away, tell me where you have put him, and I will get him."
Jesus said to her, "Mary." She turned toward him and cried out in Aramaic, "Rabboni!" (which means "Teacher").
Jesus said, "Do not hold on to me, for I have not yet ascended to the Father. Go instead to my brothers and tell them, 'I am ascending to my Father and your Father, to my God and your God.'"
Mary Magdalene went to the disciples with the news: "I have seen the Lord!" And she told them that he had said these things to her.

Application

Reflect on the hope and assurance that the Resurrection of Jesus brings to your life. How does this event impact your faith journey and your understanding of God's love and power?

Consider the ways in which you can share the hope of the Resurrection with others and live in the light of this miraculous event.

Lord Teach Me To	I Am Thankful For

Prayer

Heavenly Father, thank You for the hope and assurance that the Resurrection of Jesus brings to my life. Help me to grasp the depth of Your love and power displayed in this miraculous event.

Strengthen my faith and empower me to share the hope of the Resurrection with others. May my life be a testimony to Your grace, love, and power. In Jesus' name, **Amen.**

Day 33: The Great Commission

Reflection

The Great Commission is Jesus' command to His followers to spread the Gospel to all nations, making disciples and baptizing them in the name of the Father, Son, and Holy Spirit.

As you reflect on this command, consider how you can actively participate in fulfilling the Great Commission and sharing the love of Jesus with others.

Bible Passage : Matthew 28:16-20 (NIV)

Then the eleven disciples went to Galilee, to the mountain where Jesus had told them to go.

When they saw him, they worshiped him; but some doubted.

Then Jesus came to them and said, "All authority in heaven and on earth has been given to me.

Therefore go and make disciples of all nations, baptizing them in the name of the Father and of the Son and of the Holy Spirit, and teaching them to obey everything I have commanded you. And surely I am with you always, to the very end of the age."

Application

Reflect on your role in fulfilling the Great Commission. What are some ways that you can actively share the love of Jesus and make disciples in your own life?

Consider how you can serve as a witness to others and teach them about the life-changing message of the Gospel. Pray for guidance and opportunities to share your faith with others.

Lord Teach Me To	I Am Thankful For

Prayer

Lord Jesus, thank You for the Great Commission and the privilege of being part of Your mission to share the Gospel with the world. Grant me the wisdom, courage, and opportunities to share Your love with others and to make disciples. Help me to be a faithful witness, teaching others about Your life-changing message and the hope that is found in You alone. In Your name, I pray. **Amen.**

Day 34: The Ascension

Reflection

The Ascension of Jesus marks the moment when He was taken up into heaven, after appearing to His disciples following His resurrection.

This event serves as a reminder of Jesus' promise to return one day and encourages us to anticipate His second coming.

As you reflect on the Ascension, consider how it shapes your understanding of Jesus' ministry and your own role in sharing the Gospel.

Bible Passage : Acts 1:6-11 (NIV)

So when they met together, they asked him, "Lord, are you at this time going to restore the kingdom to Israel?"

He said to them: "It is not for you to know the times or dates the Father has set by his own authority.

But you will receive power when the Holy Spirit comes on you; and you will be my witnesses in Jerusalem, and in all Judea and Samaria, and to the ends of the earth."

After he said this, he was taken up before their very eyes, and a cloud hid him from their sight.

They were looking intently up into the sky as he was going, when suddenly two men dressed in white stood beside them.

"Men of Galilee," they said, "why do you stand here looking into the sky? This same Jesus, who has been taken from you into heaven, will come back in the same way you have seen him go into heaven."

Application

Reflect on the significance of Jesus' Ascension and how it impacts your faith. Consider how it strengthens your anticipation of His second coming and encourages you to share the Gospel with others.

Pray for a deeper understanding of Jesus' ministry and for guidance in fulfilling your role as His witness.

Lord Teach Me To	**I Am Thankful For**

Prayer

Lord Jesus, thank You for Your Ascension and the promise of Your return. Help me to keep my eyes fixed on You, eagerly anticipating Your second coming. Guide me in my role as Your witness, sharing the Gospel with others and encouraging them to look forward to Your return.
Strengthen my faith and deepen my understanding of Your ministry, so that I may serve You faithfully. In Your name, I pray. **Amen.**

Day 35: The Day of Pentecost

Reflection

The Day of Pentecost marks the moment when the Holy Spirit was poured out upon the early believers, empowering them to be witnesses for Jesus and to carry out His mission.

This event demonstrates the vital role of the Holy Spirit in the life of every believer and the importance of relying on the Spirit's guidance and power. As you reflect on the Day of Pentecost, consider how the Holy Spirit is at work in your life and how you can better cooperate with the Spirit's leading.

Bible Passage : Acts 2:1-12, 36-39 (NIV)

When the day of Pentecost came, they were all together in one place. Suddenly a sound like the blowing of a violent wind came from heaven and filled the whole house where they were sitting. They saw what seemed to be tongues of fire that separated and came to rest on each of them.

All of them were filled with the Holy Spirit and began to speak in other tongues as the Spirit enabled them. Now there were staying in Jerusalem God-fearing Jews from every nation under heaven. When they heard this sound, a crowd came together in bewilderment, because each one heard their own language being spoken. Utterly amazed, they asked: "Aren't all these who are speaking Galileans? Then how is it that each of us hears them in our native language?

Parthians, Medes and Elamites; residents of Mesopotamia, Judea and Cappadocia, Pontus and Asia, Phrygia and Pamphylia, Egypt and the parts of Libya near Cyrene; visitors from Rome (both Jews and converts to Judaism); Cretans and Arabs—we hear them declaring the wonders of God in our own tongues!" Amazed and perplexed, they asked one another, "What does this mean?"

"Therefore let all Israel be assured of this: God has made this Jesus, whom you crucified, both Lord and Messiah." When the people heard this, they were cut to the heart and said to Peter and the other apostles, "Brothers, what shall we do?" Peter replied, "Repent and be baptized, every one of you, in the name of Jesus Christ for the forgiveness of your sins. And you will receive the gift of the Holy Spirit. The promise is for you and your children and for all who are far off—for all whom the Lord our God will call."

Application

Reflect on the significance of the Day of Pentecost and the role of the Holy Spirit in your life. How can you better cooperate with the Spirit's guidance and power?

Pray for a deeper understanding of the Holy Spirit's work and for the ability to discern the Spirit's leading in your daily life.

Lord Teach Me To	I Am Thankful For

Prayer

Heavenly Father, thank You for the gift of the Holy Spirit, poured out on the Day of Pentecost and given to all who believe. Help me to better understand the Spirit's work in my life and to cooperate with the Spirit's guidance and power. Teach me to discern the Spirit's leading in my daily life, and grant me the courage to follow where the Spirit leads.
In Jesus' name, I pray. **Amen.**

Day 36: Paul's Conversion

Reflection

Paul's conversion on the road to Damascus is a powerful testimony to the transformative power of Jesus Christ.

This event marked a dramatic change in Paul's life, as he went from persecuting Christians to becoming one of the most influential apostles and spreading the gospel throughout the known world.

As you reflect on Paul's conversion, consider how Jesus has transformed your life and how you can share the hope and love of Christ with others.

Bible Passage : Acts 9:1-20 (NIV)

Meanwhile, Saul was still breathing out murderous threats against the Lord's disciples.
He went to the high priest and asked him for letters to the synagogues in Damascus, so that if he found any there who belonged to the Way, whether men or women, he might take them as prisoners to Jerusalem.

As he neared Damascus on his journey, suddenly a light from heaven flashed around him. He fell to the ground and heard a voice say to him, "Saul, Saul, why do you persecute me?" "Who are you, Lord?" Saul asked. "I am Jesus, whom you are persecuting," he replied.
"Now get up and go into the city, and you will be told what you must do."

The men traveling with Saul stood there speechless; they heard the sound but did not see anyone. Saul got up from the ground, but when he opened his eyes he could see nothing. So they led him by the hand into Damascus. For three days he was blind, and did not eat or drink anything.

In Damascus there was a disciple named Ananias.
The Lord called to him in a vision, "Ananias!" "Yes, Lord," he answered.
The Lord told him, "Go to the house of Judas on Straight Street and ask for a man from Tarsus named Saul, for he is praying.
In a vision he has seen a man named Ananias come and place his hands on him to restore his sight."

"Lord," Ananias answered, "I have heard many reports about this man and all the harm he has done to your holy people in Jerusalem.
And he has come here with authority from the chief priests to arrest all who call on your name."

But the Lord said to Ananias, "Go! This man is my chosen instrument to proclaim my name to the Gentiles and their kings and to the people of Israel. I will show him how much he must suffer for my name."
Then Ananias went to the house and entered it.

Placing his hands on Saul, he said, "Brother Saul, the Lord—Jesus, who appeared to you on the road as you were coming here—has sent me so that you may see again and be filled with the Holy Spirit."

Immediately, something like scales fell from Saul's eyes, and he could see again. He got up and was baptized, and after taking some food, he regained his strength.
Saul spent several days with the disciples in Damascus.
At once he began to preach in the synagogues that Jesus is the Son of God.

Application

Reflect on the story of Paul's conversion and how Jesus has transformed your life. How can you share the hope and love of Christ with others in your daily interactions?

Pray for opportunities to be a witness for Jesus and for the boldness to share your faith with others.

Prayer

Lord Jesus, thank You for the transformative power of Your love and grace, as demonstrated in the life of Paul. Help me to share Your hope and love with others in my daily interactions, just as Paul did after his encounter with You.
Grant me the courage to be a bold witness for You, and open my eyes to the opportunities You provide for me to share my faith with others. May my life be a testimony to the incredible work You can do in the hearts and lives of those who surrender to You. In Your holy name, I pray. **Amen.**

Day 37: The Early Church

Reflection

The early church was marked by unity, devotion to the apostles' teachings, and a strong sense of community.

As you read about the early church, consider how these attributes can be applied to your own faith community and personal walk with God.

Bible Passage : Acts 2:42-47, 4:32-37 (NIV)

They devoted themselves to the apostles' teaching and to fellowship, to the breaking of bread and to prayer.

Everyone was filled with awe at the many wonders and signs performed by the apostles. All the believers were together and had everything in common. They sold property and possessions to give to anyone who had need.

Every day they continued to meet together in the temple courts. They broke bread in their homes and ate together with glad and sincere hearts, praising God and enjoying the favor of all the people.

And the Lord added to their number daily those who were being saved.

All the believers were one in heart and mind. No one claimed that any of their possessions was their own, but they shared everything they had. With great power the apostles continued to testify to the resurrection of the Lord Jesus.

And God's grace was so powerfully at work in them all that there were no needy persons among them. For from time to time those who owned land or houses sold them, brought the money from the sales and put it at the apostles' feet, and it was distributed to anyone who had need.

Joseph, a Levite from Cyprus, whom the apostles called Barnabas (which means "son of encouragement"), sold a field he owned and brought the money and put it at the apostles' feet.

Application

Reflect on the unity, devotion, and sense of community that characterized the early church. How can you foster these attributes in your own faith community and personal walk with God?

Pray for guidance in contributing to the growth of your faith community and in supporting one another in love, just as the early church did.

Lord Teach Me To	**I Am Thankful For**

Prayer

Heavenly Father, thank You for the example of the early church and the lessons we can learn from their unity, devotion, and sense of community. Help me to foster these attributes in my own faith community and personal walk with You. Guide me in contributing to the growth of my faith community and in supporting one another in love. May we, as Your children, work together to further Your kingdom and bring glory to Your name. **Amen.**

Day 38: The Missionary Journeys of Paul

Reflection

Paul's missionary journeys, as recorded in the book of Acts, demonstrate his unwavering commitment to spreading the Gospel and his relentless pursuit of God's calling on his life. As you read about Paul's journeys, consider the ways in which you can be an ambassador for Christ in your own life and share the Good News with others.

Bible Passage: Acts 13:1-5, 14:21-28, 16:6-15, 18:1-11 (NIV)

Now in the church at Antioch there were prophets and teachers: Barnabas, Simeon called Niger, Lucius of Cyrene, Manaen (who had been brought up with Herod the tetrarch) and Saul. While they were worshiping the Lord and fasting, the Holy Spirit said, "Set apart for me Barnabas and Saul for the work to which I have called them." So after they had fasted and prayed, they placed their hands on them and sent them off.The two of them, sent on their way by the Holy Spirit, went down to Seleucia and sailed from there to Cyprus.
When they arrived at Salamis, they proclaimed the word of God in the Jewish synagogues. John was with them as their helper.

They preached the gospel in that city and won a large number of disciples. Then they returned to Lystra, Iconium, and Antioch, strengthening the disciples and encouraging them to remain true to the faith. "We must go through many hardships to enter the kingdom of God," they said. Paul and Barnabas appointed elders for them in each church and, with prayer and fasting, committed them to the Lord, in whom they had put their trust. After going through Pisidia, they came into Pamphylia,and when they had preached the word in Perga, they went down to Attalia. From Attalia they sailed back to Antioch, where they had been committed to the grace of God for the work they had now completed. On arriving there, they gathered the church together and reported all that God had done through them and how he had opened a door of faith to the Gentiles. And they stayed there a long time with the disciples.

Paul and his companions traveled throughout the region of Phrygia and Galatia, having been kept by the Holy Spirit from preaching the word in the province of Asia. When they came to the border of Mysia, they tried to enter Bithynia, but the Spirit of Jesus would not allow them to. So they passed by Mysia and went down to Troas. During the night Paul had a vision of a man of Macedonia standing and begging him, "Come over to Macedonia and help us."
After Paul had seen the vision, we got ready at once to leave for Macedonia, concluding that God had called us to preach the gospel to them

From Troas we put out to sea and sailed straight for Samothrace, and the next day we went on to Neapolis. From there we traveled to Philippi, a Roman colony and the leading city of that district of Macedonia. And we stayed there several days.

On the Sabbath we went outside the city gate to the river, where we expected to find a place of prayer. We sat down and began to speak to the women who had gathered there. One of those listening was a woman from the city of Thyatira named Lydia, a dealer in purple cloth. She was a worshiper of God.

The Lord opened her heart to respond to Paul's message.
When she and the members of her household were baptized, she invited us to her home. "If you consider me a believer in the Lord," she said, "come and stay at my house." And she persuaded us.

After this, Paul left Athens and went to Corinth. There he met a Jew named Aquila, a native of Pontus, who had recently come from Italy with his wife Priscilla, because Claudius had ordered all Jews to leave Rome. Paul went to see them,and because he was a tentmaker as they were, he stayed and worked with them. Every Sabbath he reasoned in the s ynagogue, trying to persuade Jews and Greeks.

When Silas and Timothy came from Macedonia, Paul devoted himself exclusively to preaching, testifying to the Jews that Jesus was the Messiah. But when they opposed Paul and became abusive, he shook out his clothes in protest and said to them, "Your blood be on your own heads! I am innocent of it.

From now on I will go to the Gentiles." Then Paul left the synagogue and went next door to the house of Titius Justus, a worshiper of God. Crispus, the synagogue leader, and his entire household believed in the Lord; and many of the Corinthians who heard Paul believed and were baptized.

One night the Lord spoke to Paul in a vision: "Do not be afraid; keep on speaking, do not be silent. For I am with you, and no one is going to attack and harm you, because I have many people in this city."
So Paul stayed in Corinth for a year and a half, teaching them the word of God.

Application

As you reflect on the missionary journeys of Paul, consider the perseverance and dedication he showed in spreading the Gospel despite numerous challenges and opposition. Think about your own life and how you can be more committed to sharing your faith with others.

What opportunities can you take advantage of to share the message of Jesus with those around you? Pray for guidance and boldness to seize these opportunities and share your faith.

Lord Teach Me To

I Am Thankful For

Prayer

Heavenly Father, thank You for the inspiring example of Paul's missionary journeys. Help me to learn from his dedication and perseverance in spreading the Gospel. Give me the courage and wisdom to share my faith with those around me, and help me to seize the opportunities that come my way. Strengthen my commitment to You and empower me to be a witness of Your love and grace in my everyday life. In Jesus' name, **Amen.**

Day 39: The Fruit of the Spirit

Reflection

The Fruit of the Spirit, as described by the Apostle Paul in his letter to the Galatians, is a set of virtues and character traits that should be evident in the life of every believer.

As you read and reflect on this passage, consider how these qualities can be cultivated in your own life through a deepening relationship with the Holy Spirit. Assess which of these fruits you may need to focus on more, and ask God to help you grow in those areas.

Bible Passage : Galatians 5:22-26 (NIV)

But the fruit of the Spirit is love, joy, peace, patience, kindness, goodness, faithfulness, gentleness, and self-control. Against such things there is no law.

Those who belong to Christ Jesus have crucified the flesh with its passions and desires.

Since we live by the Spirit, let us keep in step with the Spirit.

Let us not become conceited, provoking and envying each other.

Application

Reflect on the Fruit of the Spirit and how these qualities can be cultivated in your life. Assess which fruits you may need to focus on more, and ask God to help you grow in those areas.

Pray for the guidance and empowerment of the Holy Spirit to develop these character traits in your life.

Lord Teach Me To	I Am Thankful For

Prayer

Gracious God, thank You for the gift of the Holy Spirit and the guidance it provides in my life.
I ask You to help me cultivate the Fruit of the Spirit in my life. Show me the areas where I need growth and give me the strength and wisdom to develop these character traits.
May my life be a testimony to Your work within me, and may the Fruit of the Spirit be evident in all I do. In Jesus' name, **Amen.**

Day 40: The Second Coming of Christ

Reflection

The Second Coming of Christ is a major theme throughout the New Testament, and it serves as a reminder that Jesus will one day return to establish His eternal Kingdom.

As you read and reflect on this passage, consider how the anticipation of Christ's return can shape your daily life, priorities, and actions.

How can you live in a way that demonstrates your readiness for His return and commitment to His teachings?

Bible Passage : Matthew 24:36-44 (NIV)

"But about that day or hour no one knows, not even the angels in heaven, nor the Son, but only the Father. As it was in the days of Noah, so it will be at the coming of the Son of Man.

For in the days before the flood, people were eating and drinking, marrying and giving in marriage, up to the day Noah entered the ark; and they knew nothing about what would happen until the flood came and took them all away.

That is how it will be at the coming of the Son of Man.
Two men will be in the field; one will be taken and the other left.
Two women will be grinding with a hand mill; one will be taken and the other left. "Therefore keep watch, because you do not know on what day your Lord will come.

But understand this: If the owner of the house had known at what time of night the thief was coming, he would have kept watch and would not have let his house be broken into.
So you also must be ready, because the Son of Man will come at an hour when you do not expect him."

Application

Reflect on the Second Coming of Christ and how the anticipation of His return can shape your daily life, priorities, and actions.

How can you live in a way that demonstrates your readiness for His return and commitment to His teachings?

Pray for the wisdom and guidance to live a life that is pleasing to God and prepared for Christ's return.

Lord Teach Me To	I Am Thankful For

Prayer

Heavenly Father, thank You for the promise of Jesus' Second Coming. Help me to live each day with anticipation and readiness for His return. Guide my actions and priorities so that I may be a faithful servant, living in accordance with Your teachings.

Grant me the wisdom to recognize the signs of the times and the courage to share the Gospel with those around me. In Jesus' name, **Amen.**

Week 1: Creation to the Fall

Weekly Reflection

Reflect on the stories you read this week, from the creation of the world to the fall of humanity. How do these stories demonstrate God's power, creativity, and love for His creation?

Consider the consequences of sin and how it has affected humanity's relationship with God. In what ways do you see God's grace and plan for redemption throughout these early biblical accounts?

Journal Prompt

Write about your personal experience with sin and the impact it has had on your life.

How have you experienced God's grace and forgiveness, and how can you grow in your relationship with Him?

_____

_____

_____

_____

_____

_____

_____

_____

_____

_____

_____

_____

Week 2: The Patriarchs

Weekly Reflection

This week, you read about the lives of the patriarchs: Abraham, Isaac, Jacob, and Joseph. Reflect on the ways God worked through these men, despite their weaknesses and flaws. How did God remain faithful to His promises, even when they made mistakes or faced challenges?

Consider how their stories can encourage you in your own faith journey.

Journal Prompt

Choose one of the patriarchs and write about a lesson you can learn from his life.

How can you apply this lesson to your own life and faith journey?

_____
_____
_____
_____
_____
_____
_____
_____
_____
_____
_____
_____
_____
_____

Week 3: The Exodus and the Law

Weekly Reflection

Reflect on the story of the Exodus, God's deliverance of the Israelites from Egypt, and the giving of the Ten Commandments. How do these events demonstrate God's power, love, and desire for a relationship with His people? Consider the importance of the Law in guiding the Israelites and establishing their covenant relationship with God. How can the Ten Commandments help you grow in your own relationship with God?

Journal Prompt

Write about a time when you experienced God's deliverance or guidance in your life.

How did this experience strengthen your faith and deepen your relationship with Him?

Week 4: The Judges and Kings

Weekly Reflection

Reflect on the stories of the judges and kings of Israel. How do these leaders demonstrate both the best and worst of human nature?

Consider the ways God worked through them, even when they failed or turned away from Him. How can their stories inspire you to seek God's guidance and wisdom in your own life?

Journal Prompt

Choose one of the judges or kings and write about a lesson you can learn from his or her life.

How can you apply this lesson to your own life and faith journey?

Week 5: The Prophets and the Coming Messiah

Weekly Reflection

Reflect on the messages of the prophets and their role in warning, encouraging, and guiding the people of Israel. How did their words point to the coming Messiah and the hope of salvation for all people?

Consider the ways Jesus fulfilled these prophecies and how His life, death, and resurrection provide hope and redemption for all who believe in Him.

Journal Prompt

Write about a passage or prophecy from one of the prophets that has had a significant impact on your faith.

How does this passage point to Jesus, and how does it provide hope and encouragement for your own faith journey?

_____
_____
_____
_____
_____
_____
_____
_____
_____
_____
_____
_____
_____
_____

Week 6: Jesus' Life, Death, and Resurrection

Weekly Reflection

Reflect on the life, death, and resurrection of Jesus, and the impact His ministry has had on the world. Consider the ways Jesus' teachings, miracles, and parables have shaped your understanding of God's love, grace, and forgiveness.

How has the reality of Jesus' resurrection transformed your life and given you hope for the future?

Journal Prompt

Write about your personal relationship with Jesus, how it has grown throughout this 40-day journey, and how His life, death

Day : _____

Reflection

_____
_____
_____
_____
_____
_____
_____
_____
_____

Bible Passage : _____

_____
_____
_____
_____
_____
_____
_____
_____
_____
_____
_____
_____
_____
_____
_____

Application

Lord Teach Me To

I Am Thankful For

Prayer

Day : _____

Reflection

_____
_____
_____
_____
_____
_____
_____
_____
_____

Bible Passage : _____

_____
_____
_____
_____
_____
_____
_____
_____
_____
_____
_____
_____
_____
_____

Application

Lord Teach Me To

I Am Thankful For

Prayer

Day : _____

Reflection

_____
_____
_____
_____
_____
_____
_____
_____

Bible Passage : _____

_____
_____
_____
_____
_____
_____
_____
_____
_____
_____
_____
_____
_____
_____

Application

Lord Teach Me To

I Am Thankful For

Prayer

Day : _____

Reflection

_____
_____
_____
_____
_____
_____
_____
_____
_____

Bible Passage : _____

_____
_____
_____
_____
_____
_____
_____
_____
_____
_____
_____
_____
_____
_____

Application

Lord Teach Me To

I Am Thankful For

Prayer

Day : _____

Reflection

_____
_____
_____
_____
_____
_____
_____
_____
_____

Bible Passage : _____

_____
_____
_____
_____
_____
_____
_____
_____
_____
_____
_____
_____
_____
_____
_____

Application

___

Lord Teach Me To

I Am Thankful For

Prayer

Day : _____

Reflection

_____
_____
_____
_____
_____
_____
_____
_____
_____
_____

Bible Passage : _____

_____
_____
_____
_____
_____
_____
_____
_____
_____
_____
_____
_____
_____
_____
_____
_____

Application

Lord Teach Me To	I Am Thankful For

Prayer

Day: _____

Reflection

_____
_____
_____
_____
_____
_____
_____
_____
_____

Bible Passage: _____

_____
_____
_____
_____
_____
_____
_____
_____
_____
_____
_____
_____
_____
_____

Application

Lord Teach Me To	I Am Thankful For

Prayer

Day: _____

Reflection

_____
_____
_____
_____
_____
_____
_____
_____
_____

Bible Passage: _____

_____
_____
_____
_____
_____
_____
_____
_____
_____
_____
_____
_____
_____
_____

Application

Lord Teach Me To	I Am Thankful For

Prayer

Day : _____

Reflection

_____
_____
_____
_____
_____
_____
_____
_____
_____

Bible Passage : _____

_____
_____
_____
_____
_____
_____
_____
_____
_____
_____
_____
_____
_____
_____
_____

Application

Lord Teach Me To

I Am Thankful For

Prayer

Day : _____

Reflection

_____
_____
_____
_____
_____
_____
_____
_____
_____

Bible Passage : _____

_____
_____
_____
_____
_____
_____
_____
_____
_____
_____
_____
_____
_____
_____

Application

Lord Teach Me To

I Am Thankful For

Prayer

Day: _____

Reflection

_____
_____
_____
_____
_____
_____
_____
_____
_____
_____

Bible Passage: _____

_____
_____
_____
_____
_____
_____
_____
_____
_____
_____
_____
_____
_____
_____
_____

Application

Lord Teach Me To

I Am Thankful For

Prayer

Day : _____

Reflection

_____
_____
_____
_____
_____
_____
_____
_____
_____
_____

Bible Passage : _____

_____
_____
_____
_____
_____
_____
_____
_____
_____
_____
_____
_____
_____
_____
_____
_____

Application

Lord Teach Me To

I Am Thankful For

Prayer

Day : _____

Reflection

_____
_____
_____
_____
_____
_____
_____
_____
_____

Bible Passage : _____

_____
_____
_____
_____
_____
_____
_____
_____
_____
_____
_____
_____
_____
_____

Application

Lord Teach Me To

I Am Thankful For

Prayer

A Journey of Transformation

Over the past **40 days**, we have journeyed together through the Bible, exploring the stories of God's people and discovering the depths of God's love, grace, and wisdom. From the beginning of creation to the promise of Jesus' return, the Bible reveals God's overarching plan for redemption and His deep desire for a relationship with each of us.

As we reflect on this journey, it is important to recognize the transformation that has taken place within our hearts and minds.
The power of God's Word is not simply in the knowledge it imparts, but in the way it changes us and molds us into the image of Christ. Through the daily devotionals, prayers, and reflections, we have opened ourselves up to the transformative work of the Holy Spirit, allowing Him to shape our understanding and application of God's truth in our lives.

The Road Ahead

Though our **40-day** journey has come to an end, our lifelong journey with God is only just beginning. As we continue to study the Bible, pray, and seek the guidance of the Holy Spirit, our relationship with God will continue to deepen and flourish. It is important to remember that we are never alone in our walk with God. He has given us the gift of His Spirit and the fellowship of other believers to support, encourage, and challenge us along the way.

As you move forward in your faith journey, consider some practical steps you can take to continue growing in your relationship with God.
This may include setting aside regular time for Bible study and prayer, joining a small group or Bible study at your church, or seeking out opportunities to serve and share the love of Christ with others.

Living Out God's Word

Throughout this journey, we have seen how God's Word is not only meant to inform, but also to transform. As we continue to grow in our understanding of the Bible, it is crucial that we put into practice the truths we have learned. As James 1:22 reminds us, "Do not merely listen to the word, and so deceive yourselves. Do what it says."

Let the stories, lessons, and principles we have studied over these **40 days** become a foundation for our daily lives. As we strive to live out God's Word, we will become more like Jesus and experience the fulfillment, peace, and joy that come from a life surrendered to God.

A Final Prayer

Heavenly Father, thank You for the incredible journey we have taken together through Your Word over the past **40 days**. We are grateful for the insights, wisdom, and transformation You have brought into our lives as we have sought to know You more deeply and intimately.

As we continue to walk with You, we ask that Your Holy Spirit would guide us in truth, empower us to live out Your Word, and help us to grow in our relationship with You. May our lives be a testimony to Your love, grace, and mercy, and may we continually seek to know You more and more each day.

In the precious name of Jesus, we pray. Amen.

Thank you, Faith Shepherd

Faith Shepherd's books offer a powerful and inspiring message of hope, faith, and love. Her books are perfect for those seeking to deepen their spiritual journey and grow in their relationship with God.

Through her insightful and thought-provoking writing, **Faith Shepherd** shares practical wisdom and guidance for living a more purposeful and fulfilling life.

If you're looking for uplifting and inspiring reading material, don't hesitate to check out Faith Shepherd's books!

Pray With Faith
Week 1: Personal Needs
Week 2: Family Needs
Week 3: Friends Needs
Week 4: Community Needs
Week 5: Nation Needs
Week 6: World Needs
Week 7: Church Needs
Week 8: Spiritual Needs
Week 9: Emotional Needs
Week 10: Physical Needs
Week 11: Financial Needs
Week 12: Relationship Needs

ASIN: B0C1J1MX25

Lord, Teach Me To Pray
Week 1: Humility
Week 2: Patience
Week 3: Love
Week 4: Faithfulness
Week 5: Wisdom
Week 6: Forgiveness
Week 7: Gratitude
Week 8: Courage
Week 9: Strength
Week 10: Hope
Week 11: Perseverance
Week 12: Trust

ASIN: B0C1JJV7WH

My Prayer Journal Grateful Heart
Week 1: Family
Week 2: Friends
Week 3: Health
Week 4: Home
Week 5: Job/Career
Week 6: Finances
Week 7: Opportunities
Week 8: Education
Week 9: Community
Week 10: Freedom
Week 11: Nature
Week 12: Salvation

ASIN: B0C1JGKSMJ

Copyright © Faith Shepherd, 2023